KINGDOM vs. KIN

Apostolic Identity Beyond Natural Bloodlines

By
Christopher K. Turney

Copyright Page

ISBN: 979-8-9943976-1-9
Printed in the United States of America

DEDICATION

To the family of God, the eternal household that transcends bloodlines and generations, where the Father's will unites us, the Son's love redeems us, and the Spirit's power equips us.

And to those who have chosen Kingdom purpose above personal comfort, your obedience inspires this work.

ACKNOWLEDGEMENTS

This book was born out of years of observing, praying over, and wrestling with the tension between the natural family and the family of God.

I want to thank my spiritual sons and daughters, whose Kingdom commitment has shown me what it means to prioritize God's house while still honoring our natural households. You are proof that divine order is not only possible but powerful.

To my fellow laborers in the Kingdom, you have walked this road with me, bearing the weight of ministry while keeping your eyes on the King. Your example has sharpened my faith and strengthened my resolve.

Above all, I thank my Lord and King, Jesus Christ, who redefined family for us all and calls us to an allegiance higher than blood: to the will of the Father.

CONTENTS

PREFACE

A WORD BEFORE WE BEGIN

From the moment Adam and Eve stepped out of agreement with God, something fractured in the human family that no amount of natural wisdom, counseling, or good intention could fully mend. The relationship that once reflected the image of God, male and female united in purpose to exercise dominion, gave way to desire for control, competition for influence, and conflict of priority.

But the deepest fracture was not merely relational.
It was governmental.

The family, originally designed as a co-missional partnership under God's rule, slowly became an inward-focused system governed by familiarity rather than formation. What was meant to advance the purposes of God began to preserve comfort, protect preference, and resist transformation. Over time, the family became not just the place where God's purpose was nurtured, but also the place where His purpose was most often negotiated.

This tension did not remain in Genesis. It echoes throughout Scripture and persists powerfully in our present moment.

Today, family is often treated as the highest loyalty, the ultimate priority, and the unquestioned reference point for obedience, even within the Church. Phrases like "family first" and "my first ministry is my family" are repeated with sincerity, yet rarely examined in the full light of Scripture. As a result, the family, especially the privatized nuclear family, has quietly become a substitute for the family of God rather than an expression of it.

This book was written to confront that substitution.

It is not an attack on family.
It is a call to reorder family under the Kingdom of God.

The Kingdom does not erase family, it redeems it. But redemption requires alignment. In the Kingdom, Christ is preeminent, allegiance is clarified, love is purified of sentimentality, and every relationship finds its place beneath divine purpose rather than emotional demand.

As you read, you may be challenged to rethink assumptions you have long considered sacred. You may be confronted with ways familiarity has limited faith, how sentiment has displaced obedience, or how comfort has subtly governed calling. This is not meant to bring condemnation, but clarity.

The question this book ultimately asks is simple, but weighty:

Which family is forming you, the one you were born into, or the one you were named into?

It is my prayer that as you read, the Holy Spirit will not diminish your love for family, but deepen it, by anchoring it in sonship, obedience, and the unshakable Kingdom of God.

HOW TO READ THIS BOOK

This book is not anti-family.
It is anti-substitution.

It does not seek to diminish marriage, parenting, or household life. It seeks to restore them to their rightful place under the government of God. The tension you may feel while reading is not accidental, it is diagnostic. Whenever divine order confronts familiar assumptions, resistance is often the first response.

This book challenges ideas that have become sacred through repetition rather than revelation. Many of the beliefs surrounding family, marriage, church, and priority are culturally reinforced and emotionally defended, yet rarely examined in the light of Scripture as a whole. The goal here is not to provoke offense, but to provoke alignment.

You may encounter statements that unsettle long-held convictions, particularly the notion that the nuclear family is the highest unit of identity or that family loyalty supersedes Kingdom obedience. These ideas are not attacked for shock value; they are examined because Scripture consistently reveals something higher: the household of God.

This book is best read slowly.
Not defensively.
Not selectively.

But prayerfully.

Rather than asking, "Do I agree with this?" consider asking:

- "What assumptions am I holding that Scripture may be challenging?"
- "Where has familiarity shaped my thinking more than formation?"
- "Which family has most formed my identity, the one I was born into, or the one I was named into?"

Some chapters are confrontational by necessity. Others are restorative by design. Together, they form a single argument: God is building a family that cannot be sustained by sentiment, familiarity, or isolation, only by sonship, obedience, and shared mission.

This book does not call readers to abandon family. It calls them to submit family to the Kingdom, so it can be healed, multiplied, and sent.

If read with humility, this book will not fracture your relationships, it will reorder them.

And in that reordering, you may discover that what the Kingdom requires is not less love, but truer love, governed by the Father rather than familiarity.

INTRODUCTION

WHEN BLOODLINES COMPETE WITH THE KING'S LINE

"Your desire will be for your husband, and he shall rule over you." Genesis 3:16

Those words were not a divine endorsement of hierarchy; they were a prophetic diagnosis of the disease that entered the first family the moment the knowledge of good and evil did.

Before the fall, Adam and Eve were co-heirs, co-rulers, and co-laborers. Their partnership reflected the unity of Father, Son, and Spirit, each distinct, yet working in perfect agreement. They ruled over the fish of the sea, the birds of the air, the animals of the field, and the works of God's hands. But they were never given dominion over one another.

The fruit changed everything. In one act of disobedience, the agreement that bound them was replaced with mistrust, blame, and a battle for control. Eve's desire became tethered to Adam's approval; Adam's leadership became marked by dominance rather than service. What was once a covenant became a contest.

That cycle of competition runs like a thread through Scripture:

- Sarah and Hagar producing rival sons
- Jacob and Esau battling for a father's blessing
- Joseph's brothers selling him into slavery out of envy
- David's children rising against him to take his throne

These are not just stories, they are warnings. The very relationships meant to nurture us can also distract, detour, and even derail our obedience to God if we exalt them above His Kingdom order.

When Jesus said, "Who is My mother, and who are My brothers?" He was not rejecting His family; He was revealing the higher family. The Kingdom family, those who hear the Word and do it, is eternal. Our natural family, precious as it is, must be submitted to the greater call of God.

This book is about untangling the knots between kinship and Kingdom, honoring both while allowing neither to be misplaced. It is a journey through Scripture, history, and the human heart to discover how the Kingdom restores family from a battleground to a blessing.

PART I

The Origin of Family Dysfunction

CHAPTER 1

DOMINION WITHOUT DOMINATION: THE ORIGINAL DESIGN AND THE RISE OF FAMILIAR JUDGMENT

Before there was sin, there was order. Before there was blame, there was blessing. In the beginning, God created man and woman as His image-bearers, charging them with a shared assignment:

"Let them have dominion…" (Genesis 1:26)

Notice the language, let them. Not him over her, not her over him, but them together over creation.

Adam and Eve stood as co-heirs in God's delegated authority. Dominion was not about control over one another, but stewardship over creation. Their relationship was marked by transparency, "naked and unashamed" in body, mind, and spirit. There were no hidden agendas, no competition, and no suspicion.

The Tree That Changed Everything

In the garden stood many trees for food and delight, but two trees stood apart in significance:

- The Tree of Life
- The Tree of the Knowledge of Good and Evil

The Tree of Life was the continual source of divine order and unity. The Tree of the Knowledge of Good and Evil was the potential source of separation and independence from God. God's command was simple: do not eat of it. The warning was not arbitrary, it was protective.

For before they ate, Adam and Eve did not possess the capacity to determine good and evil on their own terms. They lived from God's voice, not from internal verdicts. There was no scale of moral self-measurement. No suspicion. No judgment.

The Serpent's Strategy

The serpent's temptation was not simply to get them to do wrong, it was to get them to think independently from God.

"You will be like God, knowing good and evil." (Genesis 3:5)

The bait was not power over creation; they already had that. It was power to be self-referential in morality. The power to define "right" and "wrong" without submission to God's authority.

When Eve ate and gave to Adam, something immediate and irreversible happened: their eyes were opened, and they knew they were naked. The nakedness wasn't new, the awareness was.

And here is the fracture: for the first time, they viewed one another through the lens of self-informed judgment rather than through the innocence of divine perspective.

The Birth of Familiar Judgment

Before the fruit, Adam had never looked at Eve and measured her. Eve had never looked at Adam and evaluated him. Now, each had become a judge, armed with a knowledge they were never created to wield.

This was not general "sin" in the abstract, it was the implantation of a judgment system. A system based on the knowledge of good and evil that would cause every relationship thereafter to be tainted by suspicion, measurement, and self-justification.

From that day forward:

- They could interpret motives without God's voice confirming them.
- They could assign guilt without perfect love guiding them.
- They could elevate themselves over the other by their own standards.

God's question in the garden reveals this shift:
"Who told you that you were naked?" (Genesis 3:11)

No one had to tell them, they told themselves. The verdict came from within.

From Co-Dominion to Competition

God's pronouncement in Genesis 3:16 was not a new law but a description of the relational fallout:
"Your desire will be for your husband, and he shall rule over you."

Desire here speaks to longing, dependence, or even manipulation; ruling speaks to dominance. The unity of partnership was replaced by a cycle of control, each justifying their position based on the knowledge they now possessed about the other.

Where there had been co-dominion over creation, there was now competition for the upper hand within the home.

The Ripple Into the Next Generation

This judgmental framework did not stop with Adam and Eve, it reproduced in their sons. Cain and Abel both brought offerings to God, but Cain, seeing Abel's offering accepted while his was not, interpreted the situation through the same corrupted lens that had been passed down.

Instead of receiving God's counsel to "rule over" the sin at his door (Genesis 4:7), Cain judged Abel as the obstacle to his acceptance. In that moment, brother became adversary, worship became competition, and jealousy birthed murder.

The contest between husband and wife in the first generation became the contest between brothers in the second.

The Lasting Effect

Every family since has been shaped by this root fracture. We judge one another not from the Tree of Life but from the knowledge of good and evil. We form opinions about family members based on history, behavior, and perceived motives, and once our verdict is set, it becomes the lens through which we interpret their every move.

The Kingdom's restoration is not simply about forgiving sin, it's about removing the false seat of judgment we took when we ate from that tree. Christ came not only to reconcile us to God but to restore us to one another, replacing suspicion with love and judgment with righteousness that flows from Him alone.

From the Tree of Knowledge Back to the Tree of Life

The entrance of judgment into the family was not the end of God's story, it was the setup for redemption. In the middle of their failure, God spoke of a Seed that would crush the serpent's head (Genesis 3:15). That Seed was Christ.

When Jesus came, He did not invite us back to the Tree of the Knowledge of Good and Evil to try again, He came to restore our access to the Tree of Life. In Him, innocence is restored, not by ignorance of sin, but by righteousness that comes from God alone.

At the cross, Christ absorbed the full weight of human judgment, both God's righteous judgment on sin and man's unrighteous judgment on one another. In doing so, He dismantled the false throne we built in our own minds, the seat where we presumed to weigh one another's worth by our own standards.

The Tree of Life, once guarded by cherubim and a flaming sword, is now opened through the pierced side of the Son of God. The same sword that kept man out has now cleared the way in.

This is why Jesus commands, "Judge not according to appearance, but judge righteous judgment" (John 7:24). True judgment is not rooted in our familiarity with someone's history, but in God's eternal perspective. In the Kingdom, we see one another "in Christ," not in Adam.

The restoration of the family, natural and spiritual, requires that we exchange the fruit of judgment for the life-giving fruit of the Spirit. It means laying down the scales we've used to measure one another and taking up the yoke of Christ, which re-centers our relationships in God's voice, not our verdicts.

What was lost in Eden was not merely obedience, it was perspective. The moment Adam and Eve ate from the tree of the knowledge of good and evil, they began to see one another through familiarity rather than formation, through memory rather than revelation. That distorted way of seeing did not remain confined to the garden; it became the inherited lens through which families, communities, and eventually entire cultures would relate to one another. The Kingdom was still God's intention, but its expression would now be resisted not only by sin, but by something far subtler:

the natural closeness that dulls honor, weakens faith, and quietly limits transformation. To understand why the Kingdom so often struggles to be demonstrated, even where truth is known, we must confront how familiarity continues to govern our relationships today.

How Familiarity Still Restricts the Kingdom Today

Familiarity continues to diminish Kingdom expression in at least four critical ways:

1. Familiarity Replaces Honor with Assumption

Honor makes room for authority.
Familiarity assumes it already understands.

In families, churches, and even marriages, familiarity says:

- "I know you."
- "I've seen you fail."
- "You're just like you've always been."

This mindset quietly resists present authority and future calling. It treats God's work in a person as incremental rather than transformative. As a result, faith is lowered, expectation is reduced, and miracles become rare.

2. Familiarity Weakens Faith and Expectation

Faith thrives on revelation. Familiarity thrives on repetition.

When people believe they already know what God will do, or won't do, faith stalls. This is why those closest to Jesus struggled most to receive from Him. They did not expect Heaven to break in because their expectations were shaped by history, not revelation.

In modern contexts, this shows up as:

- "That's just how my spouse is."
- "That's how my kids have always been."
- "That's how our family operates."
- "That's just who I am."

Familiarity locks people into static identities, while the Kingdom calls people forward.

3. Familiarity Turns Homes Inward Instead of Outward

The Kingdom is centrifugal, it moves outward.
Familiarity is centripetal, it pulls inward.

When families become overly familiar, they turn into closed systems:

- Protecting peace
- Preserving comfort
- Avoiding disruption
- Resisting sending

This inward turn suffocates Kingdom expansion. Instead of homes becoming launch points for mission, discipleship, hospitality, and apostolic sending, they become preservation units focused on maintaining normalcy.

The result is spiritual stagnation masked as stability.

4. Familiarity Replaces Formation with Tolerance

Formation requires confrontation, truth, and growth. Familiarity prefers tolerance, accommodation, and peacekeeping.

Rather than shaping sons and daughters for destiny, familiar systems adapt to dysfunction:

- Immaturity is excused
- Disobedience is explained away
- Resistance is tolerated
- Calling is delayed

In this way, familiarity does not just resist the Kingdom, it re-trains people to live beneath it.

Why the Kingdom Requires Distance from Familiarity

Jesus' call to "leave" was not abandonment, it was repositioning.

Leaving family, nets, homes, and familiarity was often necessary so identity could be formed by the Father rather than constrained by history. Distance created space for revelation, faith, and authority to grow.

This is why Kingdom advancement so often requires:

- Leaving familiar voices
- Leaving inherited expectations
- Leaving systems that know who you were

Not because family is evil, but because familiarity limits transformation.

The Restoration

The Kingdom does not eliminate relationship, it redeems it.

When family is reordered under sonship:

- Honor replaces assumption
- Faith replaces memory
- Formation replaces tolerance
- Sending replaces preservation

Only then can homes become places where the Kingdom is not merely discussed but demonstrated.

Why This Matters

Where familiarity governs, the Kingdom stalls.
Where honor leads, the Kingdom advances.

This is not just a biblical observation.
It is a present-day diagnosis.

And until familiarity is submitted to formation, the Church will continue to possess truth without power, theology without authority, and family without Kingdom demonstration.

CHAPTER 2

DESIRE AND RULE: THE FALL'S FRACTURE IN THE FAMILY

When God confronted Adam and Eve after the fruit, His words were not arbitrary punishments, they were prophetic descriptions of what life in a fallen state would look like. To the woman He said:

"Your desire shall be for your husband,
and he shall rule over you." (Genesis 3:16)

We must read this carefully. This is not God creating patriarchy, it is God diagnosing what sin has unleashed.

From Partnership to Power Struggle

Before the fall, Adam and Eve's relationship was marked by mutual purpose. They were co-missioned, two image-bearers exercising dominion outward toward creation. But now, the inward gaze had turned on each other.

The Hebrew word for "desire" here (teshuqah) is used only three times in Scripture, once here, once in Genesis 4:7 of sin's desire to master Cain, and once in Song of Solomon 7:10 of romantic longing. In this context, it's not describing healthy affection but an inordinate longing or pull toward control, dependence, or influence.

Likewise, the word "rule" (mashal) means to govern, dominate, or exercise authority over. Before the fall, Adam had no command to rule Eve. After the fall, dominance would become the default posture of men toward women, just as manipulation or over-dependence would become the default posture of women toward men.

In other words: the co-mission was replaced with a competition.

How Desire and Rule Play Out

The desire rule-cycle is destructive because it feeds on itself:

- The more one seeks control through desire, the more the other resists through dominance.
- The more one asserts dominance, the more the other responds through covert manipulation or over-dependence.

It's not just a marriage problem; it's a family culture. Children raised in this dynamic either perpetuate the same cycle or swing to the opposite extreme in their own relationships.

This is why Genesis 4 so quickly moves from marital fracture to fratricide, brother killing brother. Cain and Abel's conflict mirrors their parents', a competition for acceptance, a refusal to submit to God's counsel, and a willingness to sacrifice relationship for perceived position.

Desire and Rule in Scripture's Families

We see this broken dynamic repeatedly in the households of the Bible:

Abraham and Sarah

Sarah desired an heir, but when God's promise seemed delayed, she took control, giving Hagar to Abraham. Abraham ruled in passivity, going along instead of leading in obedience. The result was rivalry between Hagar and Sarah and conflict between Ishmael and Isaac.

Isaac and Rebekah

Rebekah desired Jacob to have the blessing, so she manipulated circumstances to deceive Isaac. Isaac, determined to rule over the decision, favored Esau. Desire and rule once again produced division in the family.

David and Michal

Michal desired David's affection, but later despised him when his worship before the ark offended her pride. David, instead of restoring relationship, distanced himself, ruling through emotional withdrawal.

In every case, desire and rule distort the original design of unity, replacing mutual trust with mutual suspicion.

Why This Fracture is So Deep

The reason Genesis 3:16 is so potent is that it goes beyond surface conflict, it points to the operating system of fallen relationships. This is why counseling, communication techniques, and conflict management alone cannot fully fix a marriage or a family. The issue is not just behavior, it's the root mindset installed at the fall.

When Adam and Eve ate the fruit, they didn't just disobey, they changed the way they saw each other. Desire and rule are simply the relational expressions of that change.

The Kingdom's Antidote

The Kingdom does not erase God-given roles, but it redeems them. In Christ, "desire" is no longer about control but about devotion, and "rule" is no longer about dominance but about self-giving leadership.

Paul writes:
"Submitting to one another in the fear of God." (Ephesians 5:21)

In the Kingdom, submission is mutual, not one ruling while the other resists, but both yielding to the will of the King.

The answer to desire and rule is not reversing the roles, it's restoring the relationship to the original order where they have dominion together. That means replacing manipulation with trust, replacing dominance with sacrificial love, and replacing suspicion with the perspective of the Tree of Life.

In the next chapter, we'll watch how this fracture in Adam and Eve's home multiplied into their children, and how the same dynamic continues to reproduce in every family that refuses the Tree of Life. Cain and Abel will stand as the first case study of how familial fracture, once rooted in judgment, blossoms into hostility, rivalry, and even violence.

CHAPTER 3

BROTHERS AT WAR: CAIN, ABEL, AND THE CYCLE OF COMPETITION

The first family after Eden was already carrying the weight of the fall. Adam and Eve had eaten from the Tree of the Knowledge of Good and Evil; their relationship was now marked by the undercurrent of desire and rule. And into that atmosphere their first sons were born.

Cain was the firstborn, a worker of the soil. Abel was the younger, a keeper of sheep. Both brought offerings to the Lord, but God looked with favor on Abel's offering and not on Cain's.

To the untrained eye, this was simply a matter of personal preference. But to Cain, who now saw life through the fractured lens inherited from his parents, it was a judgment.

The Inherited Lens

From Adam and Eve, Cain had inherited more than human nature, he had inherited a way of thinking. The knowledge of good and evil meant Cain could now interpret God's actions through his own assumptions.

Instead of asking, "Lord, what needs to change in me?" Cain asked, "Why him and not me?" The same knowledge that allowed Adam and Eve to measure one another's nakedness now allowed Cain to measure his brother's worth against his own.

In Cain's mind:

- Abel's acceptance meant his rejection.
- Abel's favor meant his loss.
- Abel's "good" meant Cain's "evil."

Once judgment entered, the verdict was inevitable: Abel must be the problem.

God's Intervention

God, in mercy, confronted Cain before the sin was complete:
"If you do well, will you not be accepted?
And if you do not do well, sin lies at the door.
And its desire is for you, but you should rule over it." (Genesis 4:7)

The language mirrors Genesis 3:16. Sin's "desire" was to control Cain, but God told him to "rule over it." This was the second time in human history God called someone to rule, not over another person, but over the force that sought to dominate them.

Cain was not powerless. He was positioned to reverse the cycle. But instead of ruling sin, **he ruled his brother.**

From Worship to Warfare

Cain lured Abel into the field and killed him. The place where offerings were made to God became the place where blood was spilled in anger. Worship became warfare, not against the serpent, but against family.

This is one of the enemy's oldest strategies: turn the battle inward. If the family can be divided against itself, it will spend its strength fighting each other instead of fulfilling its God-given dominion.

The Pattern Repeats

Cain and Abel are the prototype for a pattern that unfolds across Scripture:

- Ishmael and Isaac – The child of the flesh mocking the child of promise.
- Esau and Jacob – The elder plotting to kill the younger over a blessing.
- Joseph and His Brothers – Jealousy over favor leading to betrayal and exile.

In each case, acceptance by God or man is interpreted through the lens of competition rather than co-mission. Favor is seen as exclusive instead of inclusive, and brothers become rivals instead of partners.

Competition: The Death of Co-Mission

Co-mission, working together under a shared mandate, cannot survive in an atmosphere of competition.

Competition sees every gain for you as a loss for me. Co-mission sees your gain as our gain.

The knowledge of good and evil fuels competition because it trains us to measure ourselves against others instead of aligning ourselves with God. This is why Paul later wrote:

"They measuring themselves by themselves, and comparing themselves among themselves, are not wise." (2 Corinthians 10:12)

When comparison becomes the measure, murder becomes a possibility, not always with a weapon, but with words, withholding, and the slow killing of relationship.

God's Question

After the murder, God asked Cain,

"Where is Abel your brother?" (Genesis 4:9)

Cain's response, "I do not know. Am I my brother's keeper?", was more than defiance. It was the verbal proof that the family bond had been broken in Cain's heart. Keeper had been replaced by competitor.

In God's design, family was to be the first expression of Kingdom partnership, co-stewards over creation, co-heirs of promise, co-laborers in mission. In the fractured design, family became the first arena of rivalry.

The Kingdom's Restoration

The cycle of Cain and Abel ends only in Christ. In Him, we are no longer defined by the blood we share through Adam but by the blood He shed at Calvary. The writer of Hebrews says:

"You have come… to Jesus the Mediator of the new covenant, and to the blood of sprinkling that speaks better things than that of Abel." (Hebrews 12:22, 24)

Abel's blood cried for justice, Jesus' blood cries for mercy. Abel's blood marked the breaking of brotherhood, Jesus' blood marks its restoration.

In the Kingdom, we are reintroduced to one another not as rivals but as co-heirs. Your victory is my victory. Your blessing is my blessing. The curse of comparison is broken because the favor of God in Christ is infinite and undivided.

The Kingdom is non-diminishing in nature. When one son or daughter receives, it does not subtract from another's portion. Just as the five loaves and two fish multiplied until twelve baskets of fragments remained, so too does the Kingdom increase as it is distributed. Unlike earthly resources, which shrink when divided, the resources of heaven expand in the sharing. This means I don't lose when you win, I actually gain, because the increase of His government knows no end (Isaiah 9:7). The family of God flourishes not by competition but by participation in an ever-expanding Kingdom.

In the next chapter, we will see how this cycle didn't just play out between brothers, it infiltrated entire households. From Abraham to Jacob to David, we will trace how the fracture of desire and rule, and the competition it fuels, reshaped the destiny of families, and how God's covenant purposes prevailed in spite of it.

PART II

Bloodlines in Scripture

CHAPTER 4

ABRAHAM'S HOUSEHOLD: PROMISE, PARTIALITY, AND PAIN

When God called Abram out of Ur, He gave a promise that would shape the destiny of nations:

"I will make you a great nation; I will bless you and make your name great, and you shall be a blessing." (Genesis 12:2)

The covenant was clear, Abraham's descendants would carry the blessing. But as with Adam and Eve, the fulfillment of God's promise would be contested within the family. And at the center of the conflict was the same root we saw in Eden: desire, rule, and the knowledge of good and evil shaping human judgment.

Promise Delayed, Desire Inflamed

God promised Abraham and Sarah a son, but as the years passed, desire grew, and patience waned. Sarah, interpreting the situation through her own reasoning, concluded that the promise must be fulfilled another way:

"Please, go in to my maid; perhaps I shall obtain children by her." (Genesis 16:2)

This was not merely a suggestion; it was the desire to control the outcome. And Abraham, instead of leading his household in faith, ruled passively by compliance, agreeing to Sarah's plan without seeking God's counsel.

Hagar conceived, and immediately the family dynamic shifted.

From Co-Wives to Rivals

Hagar's pregnancy produced contempt in her eyes toward Sarah. Sarah, feeling despised, blamed Abraham:

"My wrong be upon you!" (Genesis 16:5)

The judgment lens was fully active, each person assigning blame, measuring guilt, and justifying their position. Desire had taken the form of manipulation; rule had taken the form of reactionary control.

Abraham's response?

"Indeed your maid is in your hand; do to her as you please." (Genesis 16:6)

This was abdication disguised as authority. Instead of restoring order, Abraham delegated conflict management back to the offended party, further deepening the fracture. Hagar fled, only to be met by the Angel of the Lord, who sent her back with a promise for her son Ishmael.

Two Sons, Two Sources

Ishmael, the son of the bondwoman, was born from human strategy; Isaac, the son of promise, would be born from God's intervention.

Paul would later use these two as allegories in Galatians 4, Hagar representing the covenant of slavery, and Sarah the covenant of freedom. But in the moment, for Abraham's household, these were not allegories, they were competing realities.

By the time Isaac was weaned, the tension erupted again. Sarah saw Ishmael mocking and demanded that Abraham cast out Hagar and her son (Genesis 21:9–10).

The Pain of Division

Abraham was "very displeased" at Sarah's demand. This was his son too. But God told him to listen to Sarah, not because her motives were pure, but because His covenant purpose would come through Isaac.

The separation was devastating, Hagar and Ishmael sent away, Abraham's household split. What began as a desire to fulfill God's promise faster ended with alienation, grief, and the planting of seeds of enmity that would ripple through generations.

The Pattern

In Abraham's household, we see the same Edenic fracture:

- Desire – Sarah's longing for a child leading to manipulation.
- Rule – Abraham's passive authority allowing the conflict to deepen.
- Judgment – Each party interpreting the other's actions through suspicion rather than divine perspective.

The result was not just family tension, it was the creation of two lines of descendants with deeply intertwined but often hostile destinies.

Covenant Prevails

And yet, even in the midst of fracture, God's covenant plan moved forward. Isaac, the son of promise, would carry the blessing. Ishmael, though outside the covenant line, was still blessed to become a great nation (Genesis 17:20).

This is the mystery of God's sovereignty; He can work His purposes even through our relational dysfunction. But this should never be taken as permission to ignore His order. Every shortcut in fulfilling His promise carries a cost.

Kingdom Application

In the Kingdom, faith and patience inherit the promises (Hebrews 6:12). When desire tempts us to control outcomes, and when rule tempts us to dominate or abdicate, we must return to the Tree of Life, listening for God's voice rather than leaning on our own knowledge.

Abraham's household teaches us that the promise of God can survive family fracture, but the pain of the fracture will still be felt. The better way is to trust God's timing and keep the household aligned with His order from the start.

In the next chapter, we'll see how this same pattern, favoritism, manipulation, rivalry, played out in the next generation with Jacob's household, and how it escalated into deception, exile, and decades of estrangement.

CHAPTER 5

JACOB'S HOUSE: FAVORITISM, DECEPTION, AND DIVISION

The fractures in Abraham's household did not end with him. They multiplied in the next generation. Isaac and Rebekah's marriage was not immune to the same currents of desire, rule, and judgment. Their choices would set the stage for one of the most divided family narratives in all of Scripture.

Favoritism in the Parents

Isaac favored Esau, the rugged hunter; Rebekah favored Jacob, the quiet dweller in tents (Genesis 25:27–28). This wasn't a small matter of personality preference; it was an open partiality that fractured the unity of the home.

Favoritism in a parent becomes fuel for rivalry in the children. Each child learns to measure their worth through comparison with their sibling. The knowledge of good and evil is reinforced: If one is good, the other must be less so.

Desire and Rule in Action

God had already spoken a prophetic word before the twins were born:
"The older shall serve the younger." (Genesis 25:23)

Rebekah heard it, but rather than trust God to bring it to pass, she acted to control the fulfillment. This is desire, the same pattern Sarah fell into, taking matters into one's own hands.

Isaac, aware of the prophecy, seems to have chosen to "rule" by ignoring it. He favored Esau and planned to give him the blessing anyway. This is rule expressed as stubborn resistance to God's stated order.

The Deception

When Isaac prepared to bless Esau, Rebekah acted. She instructed Jacob to disguise himself as Esau to receive the blessing meant for his brother. Jacob hesitated, not out of conviction, but out of fear of being caught.

The plan worked. Isaac blessed Jacob, but the fallout was immediate. Esau's bitterness burned into murderous intent:

"The days of mourning for my father are at hand; then I will kill my brother Jacob." (Genesis 27:41)

What began as parental favoritism escalated into open deception, fractured trust, and threats of violence, echoing the Cain-and-Abel pattern.

Division and Exile

To save Jacob's life, Rebekah sent him away to her family in Haran. Her plan to "secure" the blessing for Jacob also secured decades of estrangement between mother and son. Scripture never records them seeing each other again.

Family fracture always costs more than the instigator imagines. It never stays confined to the initial act, it multiplies into separation, distrust, and cycles that continue until confronted.

Jacob Reaps What He Sows

Jacob's years in Haran brought their own lessons. He fell in love with Rachel but was deceived by her father Laban into marrying Leah first. The deceiver became the deceived.

In his own household, favoritism resurfaced, this time toward Joseph, Rachel's firstborn. The visible sign of that favoritism, the coat of many colors, became the focal point of the brothers' jealousy and the eventual cause of Joseph's exile.

The same fractures Jacob inherited from Isaac and Rebekah, partiality, deception, rivalry, were now embedded in the next generation.

The Generational Thread

From Abraham to Jacob, the same seeds keep reproducing:

- Desire to control the outcome rather than trust God's timing.
- Rule exercised through stubbornness or dominance instead of service.
- Judgment born of favoritism, suspicion, and comparison.

These elements combined in Jacob's house to create a volatile mix, one that would scatter his sons and nearly destroy the family altogether.

God's Redemptive Thread

And yet, in the midst of all the fracture, God's covenant purpose moved forward. The very son rejected by his brothers, Joseph, would one day become the one who preserved them all from famine.

This is the paradox of grace: God weaves redemption even from the threads of human dysfunction. But His grace does not make the dysfunction harmless, it still leaves scars, and the cycle will repeat unless broken.

Kingdom Application

The Kingdom family is called to break the cycles of favoritism, deception, and division. This means:

- Seeing one another through the Spirit, not through the knowledge of good and evil.
- Trusting God's word to come to pass without manipulation.
- Refusing to weaponize preference or position.

In the Kingdom, blessing is not a limited commodity. We are co-heirs, not competitors. If God exalts your brother, it is not a demotion for you, it is an elevation for the family.

In the next chapter, we will see how the same fractured dynamics found their way into the house of David, this time played out on the stage of national leadership, where family loyalty, political power, and Kingdom purpose collided.

CHAPTER 6

DAVID'S HOUSE: AFFECTION, AUTHORITY, AND REBELLION

David, Israel's shepherd-king, was a man after God's own heart (1 Samuel 13:14). He loved God deeply, worshiped freely, and ruled courageously. Yet when it came to his own household, the same fracture patterns we have traced from Eden through Abraham and Jacob were alive and well.

His story reveals that spiritual greatness in the public arena does not automatically translate to spiritual health in the private one. The same themes of desire, rule, favoritism, and judgment, and their destructive effects, are present in David's house.

Affection Without Alignment

David's love for his children was deep, but often it was unchecked by the discipline and accountability necessary to form them in righteousness. This imbalance, affection without alignment, created a vacuum in which rebellion could flourish.

One of the clearest examples is Amnon, David's firstborn. Consumed by lust for his half-sister Tamar, Amnon devised a scheme to lure her into his room. When his desire was fulfilled, his "love" turned instantly to hatred (2 Samuel 13:15). Tamar was violated and shamed.

David was "very angry" when he heard of it (2 Samuel 13:21), but he took no recorded action against Amnon. Whether out of partiality for his firstborn, personal guilt over his own past sins, or fear of division, David's inaction left a wound unhealed and justice unmet.

Rebellion in the Shadows

Tamar's full brother Absalom, outraged at David's passivity, took matters into his own hands. He harbored silent hatred toward Amnon for two years before killing him in revenge.

Absalom then fled to Geshur for three years. When he finally returned to Jerusalem, David refused to see him for another two years (2 Samuel 14:28). This prolonged estrangement deepened the fracture between father and son.

When Absalom was finally brought before David, the reconciliation was superficial. There was no confrontation of sin, no restoration of trust, only an outward gesture of peace. Absalom's heart remained alienated, and his ambition began to grow.

The Rise of Absalom

Absalom's rebellion unfolded slowly but strategically:

- Charm and Manipulation – He positioned himself at the city gate, intercepting those who came to the king

for judgment, subtly undermining David's leadership.
- Gathering Allies – Over time, he "stole the hearts of the men of Israel" (2 Samuel 15:6).
- Open Revolt – Declaring himself king in Hebron, Absalom forced David to flee Jerusalem.

The fracture had moved from private family dysfunction to public national crisis.

The Cost of Misaligned Affection

David loved Absalom to the end. Even in battle, he commanded his men to "deal gently for my sake with the young man Absalom" (2 Samuel 18:5). When Absalom was killed despite these orders, David wept bitterly:

"O my son Absalom, my son, my son Absalom,
If only I had died in your place!
O Absalom my son, my son!" (2 Samuel 18:33)

David's grief was real, but it was grief over a loss that might have been avoided had affection been balanced with authority and alignment. Love without order is like a river without banks, it may be deep, but it cannot direct life.

The Pattern in David's House

In David's household we see:

- Desire – Amnon's lust and Absalom's ambition.
- Rule – David's passive authority and eventual reactionary measures.

- Judgment – Children interpreting one another's and their father's actions through suspicion and rivalry.

This was not a lack of love, it was a misalignment of love with God's order.

Kingdom Application

The Kingdom calls fathers and mothers to love deeply but lead decisively. Affection must be joined with alignment, nurturing must be joined with accountability. The heart of God is both tender and firm, merciful and just.

When leaders, whether in a home, church, or nation, allow affection to overrule correction, they risk enabling the very rebellion that will later grieve them.

In the Kingdom, our first loyalty is to God's order, not to sentiment. When family relationships threaten to compromise divine alignment, love demands that we address, confront, and restore, not ignore, delay, or pacify.

PART III

The Kingdom's Redefinition of Family

CHAPTER 7

JESUS AND KINSHIP: THE HIGHER HOUSEHOLD

Jesus did not merely preach the Kingdom, He embodied it. Everything He said, every relationship He touched, and every boundary He challenged served one purpose: to reveal the household of His Father. And in doing so, He redefined the very concept of family.

He confronted not only sin and religion, but the privatization of family, the idea that natural households were primary, supreme, or ultimate in identity. Jesus did not weaken family; He repositioned it beneath a greater allegiance: the Father's will.

A Shocking Redefinition

One day, as Jesus was teaching, someone interrupted Him to deliver a message:

"Your mother and Your brothers are standing outside and wish to speak with You." (Matthew 12:47)

In Jewish culture, this was a moment of obligation. Family was sacred, central, and unquestioned. But Jesus responded with a Kingdom answer that stunned the crowd, and still offends religious sentiment today:

"Who is My mother, and who are My brothers?

Whoever does the will of My Father in heaven is My brother and sister and mother." (Matthew 12:48–50)

Jesus was not severing ties with Mary or His siblings, He was revealing a truth the fall had obscured:

The Kingdom forms a new family, and that family outranks biological bonds. A new household was emerging, not built on bloodline, culture, sentiment, or tradition, but on obedience to the Father.

Father Is a Family Identity, Not a Religious One

For Israel, "God" was a title.
For the Pharisees, "God" was an institution.
But for Jesus, "Father" was identity.

When He taught the disciples to pray "Our Father," He wasn't teaching a formula, He was revealing a family.

Fatherhood anchor's identity. Sonship defines relationship. This is why Jesus never said "my servant who is in heaven" or "my deity who is above." He said Father.

Wherever the revelation of the Father is embraced, a new kind of family emerges, one not shaped by competition like Cain and Abel, favoritism like Jacob's house, or rebellion like David's house, but shaped by the Father's heart.

The Higher Household

Jesus spoke frequently about "My Father's house."

But He wasn't talking about a physical building.
Not the temple.
Not a nuclear home.
Not a natural household with traditional boundaries.

He was talking about the Father's family, the spiritual household governed by covenant, identity, alignment, and mission.

This household is:

- Intergenerational, because God is the God of Abraham, Isaac, and Jacob.
- Interconnected, because believers are living stones joined together.
- Interdependent, because no member functions in isolation.
- Inter-relational, because unity is the atmosphere where glory dwells.

It's the household where Christ is the firstborn among many brethren (Romans 8:29).

The Cost of Kingdom Kinship

When Jesus called the disciples, including married men like Peter, James, and possibly others, He did not offer them a balance between home and ministry. He offered them a cross.

"If anyone comes to Me and does not hate his father and mother, wife and children… he cannot be My disciple." (Luke 14:26)

Again, this was not hatred of people, it was hatred of misalignment.

Jesus demanded the dismantling of every loyalty that competes with Kingdom allegiance.

This is why disciples left:

- Boats
- Jobs
- Extended families
- Familiar surroundings
- Inherited expectations

Not as abandonment, but as alignment to a greater household. The Kingdom does not destroy natural family; it orders it under the Father's will.

Nuclear Family vs. Kingdom Family

The nuclear family was never meant to be a closed system. In its fallen form it becomes:

- A place of private control
- A refuge from accountability
- A container of preference and personality
- A boundary that excludes spiritual community

But in the Kingdom:
Family does not shrink; it expands.

Households become open doors to community, discipleship, hospitality, and alignment. The nuclear family can easily become a unit where members influence, pressure, or limit one another according to personal will. But the household of God is directed by Him alone. No member gets to redraw boundaries; the Father sets them.

This is why Jesus did not submit His calling to the preferences of Mary or His brothers. His allegiance was to the higher household, the will of His Father.

Revelation: Family Is Assignment, Not Identity

Jesus did not reject His natural family; He restored its purpose. His mother was honored. His brothers later believed. His family was included in Kingdom purpose. But their relationship to Him shifted **from biological priority to Kingdom partnership.**

This is our pattern:
Family is God-given, but Kingdom family is God-governed.

Your natural family gives you history.
God's family gives you destiny.

Your home gives you origin.
God's household gives you purpose.

The highest loyalty is always to the Father's will, not to the expectations of a natural system that may or may not align with Kingdom purpose.

The Higher Household Is the Healthier Household

When Jesus redefined family, He wasn't diminishing it, He was redeeming it.

In the Father's household:

- There is mutual submission.
- There is shared mission.
- There is alignment to truth.
- There is accountability.
- There is community.
- There is sonship.

This is the household that hell cannot prevail against.

This is the family that cannot be fractured. This is the kinship that outlasts bloodlines and endures into eternity.

CHAPTER 8

SENTIMENTALITY VS. SPIRITUALITY: WHEN LOVE BECOMES IDOLATRY

One of the most subtle and destructive enemies of Kingdom alignment is not sin in its obvious form, it is sentiment. Not carnality, but emotional loyalty misaligned with divine priority. Sentimentality often wears the cloak of love, compassion, sensitivity, and obligation. But when it takes the lead over obedience, sentiment becomes idolatry.

In families shaped by the fall, love can easily drift into sentiment; and sentiment, left unchecked, becomes an unspoken authority that rivals the voice of God.

In the Kingdom, love submits, but sentiment often sabotages.

The Power and Danger of Human Affection

Human affection is a gift from God. We are created for connection, relationship, belonging, and deep emotional bonds. But affection becomes dangerous when it becomes governing.

Jesus confronted this directly.

In Matthew 16, after declaring Jesus to be the Christ, Peter then tried to stop Jesus from going to the cross. His affection was sincere, but it was still demonic in effect.

Jesus said:
"Get behind Me, Satan! You are not mindful of the things of God, but the things of men." (Matthew 16:23)

Peter's love for Jesus became a temptation for Jesus to avoid the will of the Father.

Sentiment opposed assignment.
Affection challenged alignment.
Love without order became a snare.

This same collision happens in households every day.

Sentimentality Defined

Sentimentality is love that has lost its submission to truth. It is emotion untethered from purpose. It is affection trying to govern what only God can order.

Where love is righteous, sentimentality is soulish. Where love strengthens obedience, sentimentality weakens it.

Where love liberates, sentimentality entangles. This is why the Kingdom cannot be governed by feelings, even noble ones.

Jesus Did Not Follow Sentiment He Followed Purpose

Jesus' ministry is filled with moments where sentiment could have derailed mission:

- His mother asked Him to perform a miracle at the wedding (John 2). He responded, "Woman, what does your concern have to do with Me?"
- His brothers mocked Him about showing Himself publicly (John 7). Jesus refused to follow their timing.
- His family tried to seize Him, thinking He was "out of His mind" (Mark 3:21). Jesus did not yield.
- His closest friend Peter begged Him not to go to the cross (Matt 16). He rebuked him sharply.

In none of these moments did Jesus allow natural affection or emotional pressure to determine His obedience.

He loved His family, but He wouldn't let them lead Him. He honored Mary, but He never allowed her desires to override the Father's will. He valued His disciples, but He refused to let their fears shape His destiny.

Love was present.
Sentimentality was denied.

The Danger of Sentimental Idolatry in Modern Families

In the modern church, sentimentality has taken on a religious tone, especially through the cliché: "Your first ministry is your family."

This sounds spiritual, but it is thoroughly unbiblical.

The truth is this:
Your first ministry is the Lord Himself. Everything else flows from that alignment and returns to that allegiance.

When family is placed above calling, several distortions occur:

1. **Family Becomes an Idol Instead of an Inheritance**
   Affection becomes worship. Comfort becomes obedience. Convenience becomes decision-making.
2. **Family Becomes a Shield from Accountability**
   Sentimentality often resists correction, discipleship, and Kingdom order.
3. **Family Becomes the Primary Voice**
   Instead of seeking God's will, decisions are made based on emotional peace, personal comfort, or familial agreement.
4. **Family Becomes the Excuse for Disobedience**
   Many avoid assignment, sacrifice, or mission under the guise of "protecting the family."

Jesus confronted this kind of thinking repeatedly (Luke 9:59–62; Luke 14:26; Matt. 19:29).

The Kingdom Is Not Anti-Family, it Is Anti-Sentiment

Kingdom order does not destroy family; it purifies it.
It does not weaken love; it redeems it.
It does not diminish affection; it reorders it under truth.

When spirituality leads, affection strengthens.
When sentiment leads, affection suffocates purpose.

A Kingdom-ordered family is one where:

- Obedience comes before comfort.
- Purpose comes before preference.
- Calling comes before convenience.
- The Father's voice outranks every other voice.

This is the household Jesus modeled.

The Cross Cuts Through Sentimentality

Jesus said:
"He who loves father or mother more than Me is not worthy of Me." (Matthew 10:37)

He was not diminishing natural love, He was protecting Kingdom order. The cross cuts away every competing loyalty, not to destroy relationship, but to free it from soulish bondage.

When a believer chooses the Father's will above sentimental ties, it does not fracture the family, it redeems it. But when a believer yields to sentimentality over Kingdom obedience, they lose both, purpose and peace.

The Higher Love

Spiritual love is not less tender than sentimental love, it is more powerful. Sentiment feels deeply; love obeys deeply. Sentiment protects comfort; love protects destiny. Sentiment avoids conflict; love confronts and restores.

Jesus loved His family more than anyone could, but He refused to allow sentiment to govern Him.

This is the love that builds the household of God.
This is the love that sets sons and daughters in order.
This is the love that breaks generational cycles.
This is the love that advances the Kingdom

CHAPTER 9

SENTIMENTALITY AND THE APOSTOLIC MODEL: SPIRITUAL SONS AND DAUGHTERS

If the fall fractured family through judgment, rivalry, sentimentality, and privatization, then the Kingdom restores family through fatherhood, sonship, and apostolic alignment. Jesus did not merely redefine family in principle, He modeled how it is rebuilt. And the clearest expression of that restoration is found in the apostolic model of spiritual sons and daughters.

This chapter marks a shift.
No longer diagnosis, now design.
No longer fracture, now formation.

Family Restored Through Sending, Not Possession

Natural family often operates through possession:

- "My child"
- "My spouse"
- "My household"
- "My responsibility"

The apostolic model operates through sending.

Jesus did not gather disciples to keep them close, He gathered them to release them. He did not father them to retain control, but to impart identity and authority so they could be sent in His name.

“As the Father has sent Me, I also send you.” (John 20:21)

This is the difference between ownership and stewardship, between control and commissioning. Natural family tends to protect; apostolic family prepares. Natural family seeks safety; apostolic family releases authority.

Paul: A Father, Not a Manager

No one articulates this more clearly than Paul.

Paul did not refer to Timothy, Titus, or Onesimus as assistants, interns, or subordinates. He called them sons.

“To Timothy, a true son in the faith…” (1 Timothy 1:2)
“To Titus, a true son in our common faith…” (Titus 1:4)

Paul understood something the modern church has often lost:
Instruction alone produces students.
Impartation produces sons.

Paul did not merely teach doctrine, he transmitted life.

“For though you might have ten thousand instructors in Christ, yet you do not have many fathers; for in Christ Jesus I have begotten you through the gospel.” (1 Corinthians 4:15)

The Kingdom is not sustained by information, it is sustained by fathering.

Apostolic Family Is Built on Likeness, Not Preference

In natural families, unity is often attempted through preference:

- Shared interests
- Similar personalities
- Emotional compatibility

In apostolic families, unity is formed through likeness:

- Shared vision
- Shared doctrine
- Shared obedience
- Shared submission to Christ

This is why Paul could say:
"Be imitators of me, just as I also am of Christ." (1 Corinthians 11:1)

This is not arrogance, it is spiritual reproduction.
The goal of apostolic fatherhood is not dependency, but duplication.

Why Privatized Families Resist Apostolic Family

Privatized family models struggle with apostolic family for one primary reason:
Apostolic family removes control.

When sons and daughters are formed apostolically:

- Authority is shared, not hoarded
- Vision is inherited, not customized
- Correction is welcomed, not resisted
- Accountability is relational, not institutional

This threatens any system, natural or religious, that thrives on insulation, independence, or emotional leverage.

Apostolic family requires humility.
It requires submission.
It requires openness.
It requires trust.

And it produces maturity.

Jesus: The Pattern Son and the Pattern Father

Jesus is both the perfect Son and the perfect pattern of fathering.

As a Son:

- He lived in complete dependence on the Father
- He spoke only what He heard
- He did only what He saw

As a Father:

- He invested deeply in twelve
- He corrected directly
- He entrusted authority progressively
- He released them fully

He did not hover.
He did not shelter them from failure.
He did not build dependence on Himself.

He prepared them to live without His physical presence.

That is true fatherhood.

Spiritual Sons Are Not Employees

The modern church often replaces sons with:

- Volunteers
- Staff
- Servants
- Attendees

But sons carry the house.
Sons protect the vision.
Sons inherit responsibility.
Sons reproduce culture.

This is why Paul entrusted churches to Timothy and Titus.
This is why Jesus entrusted the Kingdom to the disciples.

Servants execute tasks.
Sons extend government.

The Household That Cannot Be Shaken

The apostolic model produces a family that is:

- Intergenerational (fathers, sons, children)
- Missional (sent, not settled)

- Aligned (doctrinally and relationally)
- Non-diminishing (authority multiplies when shared)

This is the household hell cannot fracture.

Not because it is perfect, but because it is ordered.

The Restoration of Family Through Sonship

The answer to broken homes is not stronger nuclear families. The answer is restored sonship.

When men and women know God as Father:

- They stop striving
- They stop competing
- They stop controlling
- They stop insulating

They begin to belong.
They begin to mature.
They begin to reproduce life.

This is the family Jesus is building.
This is the household the apostles established.
This is the Kingdom order being restored in the earth.

PART IV

Restoring Divine Order

CHAPTER 10

THE MYTH OF "FAMILY FIRST": WHY THE KINGDOM MUST LEAD THE HOME

Few phrases sound more virtuous in modern Christianity than "family first." It is spoken with sincerity, defended with emotion, and repeated as unquestioned wisdom. Yet despite its popularity, the phrase is neither a command of Scripture nor a principle of the Kingdom.

What makes this myth so dangerous is not that it is openly sinful, but that it sounds righteous while quietly displacing divine order.

The Kingdom of God does not operate on slogans. It operates on alignment.

Where the Phrase Came From

"Family first" did not originate in Scripture. It arose primarily as a cultural corrective, often in response to absentee fathers, overworked professionals, or abusive religious systems. While the concern was valid, the solution was misplaced.

Instead of restoring Kingdom order, the Church substituted sentiment for revelation.

The result was a theology that elevated the nuclear family above calling, obedience, and divine mission, without ever being commanded to do so by Christ or the apostles.

The Kingdom Order Is Clear

Jesus never taught family first.
He taught Kingdom first.

"Seek first the Kingdom of God and His righteousness…" (Matthew 6:33)

Jesus did not say, "Seek first your marriage," or "Seek first your children," or even "Seek first balance."

He said: Seek first the Kingdom.

Everything else finds its place only when the Kingdom is first.

Peter: A Living Rebuttal

Peter was married. Scripture confirms it clearly. Yet nowhere are we told that his wife was his "first ministry," nor are we instructed that Peter should have prioritized domestic life over the call of Christ.

When Jesus called Peter, he left his nets immediately.

Later, Peter affirmed that he traveled with his wife during ministry, not instead of it (1 Corinthians 9:5). His marriage did not compete with his calling; it was ordered under it.

Peter's loyalty was not divided, it was aligned.

The Double Standard

One of the most revealing inconsistencies in modern Christian thinking is this:

A man may work 50–60 hours a week at a secular job to provide for his family, and no one questions his priorities.

But if that same man gives himself sacrificially to the work of the Kingdom, concerns arise:

- "What about your family?"
- "You need better balance."
- "Your first ministry is at home."

Why?

Because secular labor is culturally accepted, but Kingdom obedience is spiritually threatening.

The issue is not time.
The issue is authority.

Purpose Determines Priority

The real question is not whether a person loves their family.

The real question is this:

Did I build my family around purpose, or did I choose purpose around comfort?

Marriage was never intended to be merely emotional fulfillment. It was designed to be missional compatibility.

"Can two walk together unless they are agreed?" (Amos 3:3)

When family becomes the reference point instead of the result of obedience, it ceases to function as covenant and becomes a limiter.

Jesus Was Unapologetic

Jesus said things that directly contradict the "family first" myth:

"He who loves father or mother more than Me is not worthy of Me." (Matthew 10:37)

"Whoever does not forsake all that he has cannot be My disciple." (Luke 14:33)

"Let the dead bury their own dead, but you go and preach the Kingdom of God." (Luke 9:60)

These statements are not cruel, they are clarifying.

Jesus was not attacking family.
He was attacking misordered loyalty.

Family Is Not the Enemy, Misalignment Is

The Kingdom does not diminish family; it governs it.

When the Kingdom leads:

- Family thrives
- Marriage strengthens
- Children are formed in purpose
- Homes become outposts of Heaven

When family leads:

- Calling is negotiated
- Obedience is delayed
- Sacrifice is resisted
- Destiny is domesticated

The Highest Accountability

Every believer will stand before God alone, not as a spouse, not as a parent, not as a family unit, but as a steward of calling.

"Each of us shall give account of himself to God." (Romans 14:12)

Your highest accountability is not to your family. It is to the One who called you. That accountability does not neglect family, it orders it correctly.

The Kingdom-Centered Home

A Kingdom-led home does not ask:

- "What does our family want?"

It asks:

- "What does the Father require?"

In such a home:

- God directs
- Christ governs
- The Spirit leads
- Family aligns

This is not neglect.
This is alignment.

The Truth That Frees

The myth of "family first" collapses under Scripture.

The truth is simpler, and far more liberating:

Christ first.
Kingdom first.
Purpose first.

When this order is honored, family does not lose its place, it finally finds it.

CHAPTER 11

MARRIAGE FOR MISSION: LOVE, COMPATIBILITY, AND CALLING

Marriage did not originate as a romantic solution to loneliness. It originated as a Kingdom assignment.

Before there was affection, there was purpose.
Before there was intimacy, there was mandate.
Before there was romance, there was rule.

When God said, "It is not good that man should be alone," He was not addressing emotional deficiency, He was addressing missional insufficiency. Adam did not lack companionship; he lacked a co-laborer aligned to the divine mandate. Eve was created not merely to love Adam, but to stand with him in dominion.

Marriage, at its core, is not about fulfillment, it is about formation.

Love Was Never the Foundation, Purpose Was

Modern culture teaches that marriage begins with love and is sustained by emotional compatibility. Scripture teaches something far deeper: marriage begins with calling and is sustained by covenant.

Love is vital, but love without shared direction eventually collapses under pressure. Passion fades. Circumstances change. Seasons shift. Only purpose endures.

This is why Scripture asks a question long before it celebrates romance:
"Can two walk together unless they are agreed?" (Amos 3:3)

Agreement is not preference, it is alignment.
Alignment is not chemistry; it is shared obedience.

Eve Was Not Created for Adam's Happiness

She was created for Adam's assignment.

The phrase often translated "helper suitable" (ʿēzer kenegdô) does not mean assistant or subordinate. It means strength corresponding to, one who stands face-to-face in equal force and aligned purpose.

Marriage was never intended to be hierarchical dominance or emotional dependence, it was designed as co-mission.

When marriage becomes primarily about emotional fulfillment:

- Expectations rise unrealistically
- Disappointment becomes personal
- Conflict becomes threatening
- Calling becomes negotiable

But when marriage is anchored in mission:

- Love deepens through obedience

- Conflict refines instead of fractures
- Sacrifice strengthens unity
- Purpose governs emotion

Compatibility Is Not Personality, It Is Assignment

The world defines compatibility as:

- Similar interests
- Emotional chemistry
- Personality harmony
- Shared lifestyle goals

The Kingdom defines compatibility as:

- Shared obedience
- Shared values
- Shared submission to Christ
- Shared willingness to be sent

This is why many marriages survive emotionally but stall spiritually. They love each other, but they are not walking in the same direction.

Marriage for mission does not ask:

- "Do you make me happy?"

It asks:

- "Do we help each other obey God?"

Marriage Was Never Meant to Compete With Calling

One of the great lies of modern Christianity is that marriage and calling are opposing forces.

In Scripture, marriage is not a limiter, it is a multiplier when aligned.

- Priscilla and Aquila were co-laborers with Paul.
- Peter's wife traveled with him in ministry. (1 Corinthians 9:5)
- Abraham and Sarah carried promise together (even through failure).
- Joseph and Mary stewarded the incarnation.

Marriage becomes restrictive only when it is built around comfort instead of calling.

When Love Is Asked to Replace Purpose

Many marriages collapse not because love disappears, but because love is asked to do what only purpose can sustain.

When marriage becomes:

- Identity
- Security
- Fulfillment
- Direction

…it collapses under the weight of expectation.

Marriage was never designed to save you.
Marriage was designed to serve the Kingdom with you.

The Danger of Marrying for Escape

Some marry to escape loneliness.
Others marry to escape insecurity.
Some marry to escape calling pressure.
Others marry to escape accountability.

These marriages begin with emotion, but fracture under assignment. Kingdom marriage does not escape pressure, it absorbs pressure together.

Submission Is About Alignment, Not Power

Biblical submission has been deeply misunderstood because it has been severed from purpose. Submission is not about hierarchy, it is about order under God.

"Submitting to one another in the fear of God." (Ephesians 5:21)

In Kingdom marriage:

- Both submit to Christ
- Both submit to truth
- Both submit to calling
- Both submit to growth

Authority flows not from gender, but from alignment.

Marriage as a Kingdom Witness

A marriage aligned to mission becomes:

- A testimony to the Church

- A model of sonship
- A refuge for spiritual family
- A platform for discipleship

It is not inward-focused, it is outward-facing.

Marriage was never meant to be private, it was meant to be public in purpose.

The Redemptive Truth

Marriage does not replace calling.
Calling does not diminish marriage.

When both are aligned under Christ:

- Love deepens
- Joy strengthens
- Authority multiplies
- Legacy expands

Marriage was never meant to be the goal.
Marriage was meant to be a vehicle of the Kingdom.

CHAPTER 12

FROM COMPETITION TO CO-MISSION: THE RESTORATION OF PARTNERSHIP

Everything that was fractured in Eden was not merely broken, it was misdirected. Dominion turned inward. Judgment replaced innocence. Familiarity replaced formation. Competition replaced co-mission.

But the Kingdom does not leave fractures unresolved.

The story of Scripture is not simply about redemption from sin, it is about the restoration of divine order, where sons and daughters once again stand together under one Father, advancing one purpose, sharing one mission.

What Was Lost in Eden

Adam and Eve were never meant to compete. They were never meant to rule one another. They were never meant to define good and evil for themselves. They were meant to walk together, under God, outward toward creation.

When they ate from the Tree of the Knowledge of Good and Evil:

- Dominion turned inward
- Authority became control
- Relationship became rivalry

- Family became fractured
- Familiarity became judgment

From that moment forward, every human relationship carried the seed of competition.

The Kingdom Restores What the Fall Distorted

Jesus did not come merely to forgive sin, He came to restore sonship.

"For as many as are led by the Spirit of God, these are sons of God." (Romans 8:14)

Sons do not compete.
Sons do not hoard.
Sons do not strive for position.

Sons co-inherit.

This is why the Kingdom is non-diminishing. When one son receives, the family is not diminished, it is increased.

From Rivalry to Reconciliation

In Adam, family became rivalrous.
In Christ, family becomes reconciled.

Paul declares:
"He Himself is our peace, who has made both one, and has broken down the middle wall of separation." (Ephesians 2:14)

What was once divided, Jew and Gentile Male and female, Slave and free, Brother and brother, is now reconciled into one household.

Not one hierarchy.
Not one nuclear unit.
But one family under one Father.

The Restoration of Partnership

Partnership is not equality of role, it is equality of value under divine assignment.

In the Kingdom:

- Authority flows from alignment
- Leadership serves mission
- Relationship serves obedience
- Love serves truth
- Family serves Kingdom

This is why Jesus prayed not for protection, but for unity (John 17). Unity is the atmosphere where co-mission thrives.

Marriage Restored to Co-Mission

Marriage finds its highest expression not in emotional fulfillment, but in shared obedience.

When husband and wife submit together to Christ:

- Desire loses its power to manipulate
- Rule loses its power to dominate
- Familiarity loses its power to judge

- Calling gains its power to multiply

Marriage becomes a missionary unit, not a private refuge.

The Church as Family Recovered

The early Church did not function as isolated households attending services.

They:

- Ate together
- Prayed together
- Gave together
- Were formed together
- Were sent together

They understood something modern Christianity has largely forgotten:
Family was never meant to be private, it was meant to be shared.

Co-Mission Is the Antidote

Competition says: “If you win, I lose.”
Co-mission says: “If you win, we advance.”

Competition hoards.
Co-mission releases.

Competition isolates.
Co-mission multiplies.

Competition is rooted in fear.
Co-mission is rooted in sonship.

The Household That Advances the Kingdom

The family God is restoring is not sentimental, it is strategic.
Not insulated, but integrated.
Not familiar, but formed.

A family where:

- Christ is first
- The Father is known
- Sons are sent
- Daughters are empowered
- Authority multiplies
- Mission advances

This is the household that hell cannot stop.

The Final Restoration

What Adam lost through disobedience,
Christ restored through obedience.
What familiarity fractured, sonship heals.
What competition destroyed, co-mission rebuilds.

The Kingdom does not ask us to abandon family.
It asks us to submit it, so it can be redeemed, expanded, and sent.

Conclusion

The conflict was never truly Kingdom vs. Family.

It was always:
Kingdom vs. Familiarity
Formation vs. Insulation
Sonship vs. Sentimentality
Mission vs. Preservation

When family is restored inside the Kingdom, it no longer resists God's purpose, it becomes the very vehicle through which that purpose advances.

CONCLUSION

FROM HOUSEHOLDS TO HIS HOUSEHOLD

Every generation is shaped by the families it elevates.

From the beginning, God's intent was never to produce isolated households competing for survival, identity, or control. He intended to form one family under one Father, advancing one purpose in the earth. The tragedy of the fall was not simply moral failure, it was familial fracture. Dominion turned inward. Familiarity replaced formation. Kinship began to compete with the Kingdom.

But God never abandoned His design.

From Eden to Christ, from the patriarchs to the apostles, Scripture tells a single story: God is building a household, not merely saving individuals and not sanctifying isolated families. He is forming sons and daughters who know His voice, walk in His will, and extend His rule together.

This is the family we were named into.

The Choice Before Us

Every believer must answer a sobering question:
Which family will form me?

- The family of familiarity, built on history, comfort, preference, and emotional governance?

- Or the family of God, formed by truth, obedience, sonship, and mission?

Both will claim loyalty.
Both will demand time.
Both will shape identity.

But only one advances the Kingdom.

Jesus never forced this choice, He revealed it. He did not reject natural family; He refused to allow it to rule Him. He did not diminish affection; He subjected it to obedience.

And in doing so, He showed us the way home, to the Father's household.

When Kinship Becomes a Rival Kingdom

The nuclear family was never meant to be a sovereign unit. When cultivated in isolation and governed by familiarity, it becomes a rival system, one that subtly resists transformation, avoids accountability, and prioritizes preservation over purpose.

This is not rebellion, it is substitution.

The greatest threat to Kingdom advance is rarely overt sin. It is often mis-ordered love.

When family becomes the primary reference point for obedience, calling is negotiated. When comfort becomes the measure of faithfulness, sacrifice disappears. When familiarity governs identity, formation stalls.

The Kingdom does not coexist with rival authorities, it reorders them.

The Family God Is Restoring

The family God is restoring is not sentimental, it is submitted.
Not isolated, but integrated.
Not competitive, but co-missional.
Not preserved, but sent.

It is a family where:

- The Father is known, not assumed
- Sons are formed, not managed
- Daughters are empowered, not protected from purpose
- Marriage serves mission
- Homes become outposts of Heaven
- Community replaces isolation
- Accountability is relational
- Authority multiplies through obedience

This is the household hell cannot fracture.

A Call to Realignment

The invitation of the Kingdom is not to abandon family, but to submit it. Not to reject affection, but to redeem it.

Not to diminish kinship, but to restore it inside His household.

This requires courage.

It requires letting go of familiar expectations.
It requires confronting sentimentality.
It requires choosing obedience when comfort would be easier.
It requires trusting that God's family is not a threat to ours, but its fulfillment.

The Final Word

God is not asking for divided loyalty.
He is asking for right order.

When Christ is first:

- Families are healed
- Marriages are strengthened
- Children are formed
- Communities are restored
- The Kingdom advances

The conflict was never truly Kingdom vs. Family.

It has always been:
Kingdom vs. Familiarity
Formation vs. Insulation
Sonship vs. Sentimentality
Mission vs. Preservation

Choose this day which family will form you.

As for me and my house, we will serve the Lord.

STANDALONE STUDY GUIDE

KINGDOM VS. KIN: WHEN BLOODLINES COMPETE WITH DIVINE ORDER

How to Use This Study Guide

- These questions are best engaged slowly and prayerfully.
- Journaling is strongly recommended.
- Group facilitators should allow space for silence, conviction, and dialogue.
- Not every question must be answered in one sitting.

Chapter 1 – The Fracture of Familiarity

1. How did the Tree of the Knowledge of Good and Evil alter how Adam and Eve saw one another?
2. What is the difference between innocence and familiarity?
3. How does familiarity produce judgment rather than honor?
4. In what ways can knowing someone's history limit how we expect God to work in them?
5. Where have you seen familiarity restrict faith, authority, or Kingdom demonstration in your own life or relationships?
6. Why is familiarity more dangerous than open rebellion?

7. What does it mean to submit familiarity to formation?

Chapter 2 – Brothers at War: Rivalry Born in the Home

1. How did comparison fuel the conflict between Cain and Abel?
2. Why does rivalry often begin in close relationships rather than distant ones?
3. How does competition replace co-mission in families?
4. Where do you see comparison operating in modern homes, churches, or ministries?
5. How does the Kingdom dismantle rivalry through sonship?
6. What does it look like to celebrate another's favor without fear of loss?

Chapter 3 – From Rivalry to Co-Heirs

1. What does it mean to be a co-heir in the Kingdom?
2. How does the non-diminishing nature of the Kingdom confront comparison?
3. Why does the belief that "someone else's blessing takes from mine" persist?
4. How does seeing others as rivals reveal an orphan mindset?
5. In what ways does co-heirship reshape family, church, and leadership dynamics?

6. How does Kingdom abundance free us from competition?

Chapter 4 – Households Under Strain: Covenant and Conflict

1. How did covenant purpose continue despite dysfunction in biblical households?
2. Why does God work through imperfect families rather than waiting for ideal ones?
3. How do unresolved desires and misaligned authority strain households?
4. What patterns of dysfunction repeat across generations when not confronted?
5. How does covenant differ from sentiment or tolerance?
6. What does it mean to submit family dynamics to God's covenant purposes?

Chapter 5 – Desire and Rule: When Order Is Distorted

1. How did desire and rule become distorted after the fall?
2. Why does control often replace trust in broken relationships?
3. How do power struggles manifest in modern marriages and families?
4. What is the difference between godly authority and domination?

5. How does restored sonship heal the desire-to-rule cycle?
6. Where has the Lord invited you to relinquish control?

Chapter 6 – Legacy Without Alignment

1. How did David's family illustrate the danger of affection without formation?
2. Why is unchecked familiarity often mistaken for grace?
3. How can tolerance enable rebellion rather than heal it?
4. What is the difference between protecting someone and preparing them?
5. Where does legacy fail when alignment is absent?
6. How does Kingdom accountability restore generational strength?

Chapter 7 – Jesus and Kinship: The Higher Household

1. How did Jesus redefine family?
2. What does it mean that Father is a family identity, not a religious one?
3. Why does Kingdom family supersede biological priority?
4. How does the household of God differ from the nuclear family?
5. Why does obedience determine Kingdom belonging?
6. How does embracing the higher household reshape loyalty and identity?

Chapter 8 – Sentimentality vs. Spirituality

1. How does sentimentality differ from spiritual love?
2. Why can affection become an obstacle to obedience?
3. How did Jesus confront sentiment without losing compassion?
4. Where have emotional loyalties influenced your spiritual decisions?
5. How does the crosscut through misplaced affection?
6. What does it mean to love rightly rather than sentimentally?

Chapter 9 – The Apostolic Model: Spiritual Sons and Daughters

1. What distinguishes spiritual sons and daughters from servants or volunteers?
2. Why is fatherhood essential to Kingdom formation?
3. How does impartation differ from instruction?
4. Why does privatized family resist apostolic alignment?
5. How does being "sent" reveal maturity?
6. Who has fathered or mothered you spiritually—and how?

Chapter 10 – The Myth of "Family First"

1. Where did the "family first" mindset originate culturally?
2. Why is the phrase compelling but unbiblical?
3. How does Kingdom order differ from sentimental priority?

4. Why is secular overwork often excused while Kingdom sacrifice is questioned?
5. How does purpose determine priority?
6. Where might family expectations be negotiating obedience in your life?

Chapter 11 – Marriage for Mission

1. How does Scripture define marriage differently than culture?
2. What does it mean to marry for mission rather than fulfillment?
3. How does compatibility relate to calling rather than personality?
4. Why must marriage align under purpose to thrive?
5. How can marriage multiply Kingdom impact when rightly ordered?
6. In what ways can your marriage (or future marriage) serve mission?

Chapter 12 – From Competition to Co-Mission

1. What was restored through Christ that was lost in Eden?
2. How does co-mission heal rivalry?
3. Why is sonship essential to sustained unity?
4. How does the Kingdom turn households outward again?
5. What does it mean to be formed by His household?
6. What realignment is the Holy Spirit inviting you into now?

Closing Reflection

- Which family has most shaped your identity: familiarity or formation?
- Where has God been challenging mis-ordered loyalty?
- What would it look like for your home to become an outpost of the Kingdom?

How will you respond to the call to realignment?

ABOUT THE AUTHOR

Christopher K. Turney is a Kingdom teacher, author, and apostolic leader committed to restoring biblical order, sonship, and Kingdom culture in the earth. He is the founder of Kingdom Reign Ministries, an apostolic work devoted to equipping believers to live under the government of God rather than the systems of religion, tradition, or culture.

Christopher's teaching emphasizes the revelation of God as Father, the formation of spiritual sons and daughters, and the distinction between Kingdom truth and familiar religious assumptions. With clarity and conviction, he addresses issues of identity, authority, family, discipleship, and spiritual maturity, calling believers beyond sentimentality into obedience, alignment, and purpose.

He is the author of multiple books that challenge conventional Christian thinking while remaining deeply rooted in Scripture, including works on sonship, the Kingdom of God, spiritual warfare, salvation, honor, and family. His writings are marked by theological depth, pastoral wisdom, and a passion to see the Church restored as a true household of faith rather than a collection of isolated individuals or privatized homes.

Christopher serves alongside his wife, Jill Turney, who ministers as a spiritual mother, teacher, and co-laborer in the Kingdom. Together, they lead with a shared vision to raise generations formed by truth, grounded in identity, and sent with purpose.

Christopher and Jill reside in the United States and minister both nationally and internationally through teaching, leadership development, and apostolic training.

For more information, resources, and teaching materials, visit: www.chrisandjillturney.com

SCRIPTURE INDEX

Amos

3:3 – Agreement and alignment

Malachi

4:5–6 – Turning hearts of fathers and children

Matthew

4:18–22 – The call to leave and follow
8:14–15 – Peter's household
10:34–39 – The sword and divided loyalties
12:46–50 – Jesus redefines family
16:21–23 – Sentimentality confronting assignment
19:27–29 – Leaving for the Kingdom

Mark

3:21 – Family misunderstanding Jesus
6:1–6 – Familiarity restricting miracles

Luke

9:57–62 – Kingdom priority over family obligations
14:26–33 – Allegiance and cost of discipleship

John

2:1–4 – Purpose over familiarity
7:1–9 – Family pressure and divine timing
17:20–23 – Unity and shared mission

20:21 – Sending as identity

Acts

2:42–47 – The early Church as family

Romans

8:14–17 – Sonship and co-heirship
14:12 – Personal accountability before God

1 Corinthians

4:15 – Spiritual fatherhood
9:5 – Apostles traveling with believing wives
11:1 – Imitation through alignment

2 Corinthians

5:16–17 – Knowing no one according to the flesh

Galatians

3:26–29 – Identity in Christ
6:10 – The household of faith

Ephesians

2:19–22 – Members of God's household
3:14–15 – Naming of the family of God
5:21 – Mutual submission

Colossians

1:13 – Transfer of kingdoms

Hebrews

12:7–11 – Sonship and discipline

www.ingramcontent.com/pod-product-compliance
Lightning Source LLC
LaVergne TN
LVHW010935110826
845149LV00013B/2609

9798994397619